Get Moving!

by Barbara A. Donovan

Table of Contents

The Science of Motion................ 2
Put It in Motion..................... 4
Start Moving....................... 7
Work Against Gravity 10
Keep Your Balance 13
Index 16

The Science of Motion

Do you and your friends play sports? No matter what sport you play, the science of motion helps you compete. Motion is a change from one position to another. Up, down, left, right—it's all motion.

Imagine that you're on a skateboard ramp. You stand still. Then you prepare to take off. You push with your foot and speed down the ramp.

As your skateboard moves, your speed increases. You zoom faster and faster down the ramp. Now you are really in motion!

As you go up the ramp's other side, you know that you're slowing down. Your arms steady you. The laws of motion are at work. Let's find out more about how motion works.

Put It in Motion

A gymnast is in motion the second she starts down the runway. Her speed is her rate of movement, or how fast she moves. When speed is measured as something that moves in a straight line, this is called velocity.

As the gymnast runs, her velocity changes. She starts slowly. Then, as she keeps running, she will accelerate. Accelerate means to move faster and faster.

Some motion happens in a circle. The arrows show the direction of force this athlete uses as she rotates. Her arm pulls the discus in a circle. But when she lets go, the motion of the discus will change and become a straight line.

Start Moving

Think about what happens in a game of teeball. The coach puts the baseball on the tee. Does the baseball have any speed or direction yet? No. It has no motion. It has no velocity.

When the baseball is "at rest," or sitting still on the tee, we can see a law of motion at work. This is called the law of inertia. This law says that an object at rest stays at rest until some outside force puts the object in motion. The baseball will stay at rest until someone hits it.

This golf ball is at rest on the tee. And now you know the law of inertia—the ball will stay at rest until some outside force puts it in motion. What force might that be?

Imagine that you hit the ball. THWACK! The force of your club hitting the ball works against inertia. The ball is no longer at rest. The force changes the ball's velocity—both its speed and its direction. Will the ball move through the air forever? No. Outside forces such as gravity will change its motion.

Work Against Gravity

Gravity makes things fall to Earth and stay there. Without gravity, things would be floating around—including you! When you throw or hit a ball up into the air, the ball works against gravity. The force of gravity slows the ball down though. Finally, the ball falls to the ground.

But if an astronaut in space throws a ball, it might keep going in a straight line for a long time. Why? Because there is little gravity in space. Until some other force changes the ball's motion, the ball will go on and on and on.

Suppose you shoot a basketball toward a hoop. The force from your arms and hands makes the ball accelerate. But gravity slows the ball down. As the ball reaches its highest point, gravity pulls it to Earth. SWISH! It falls through the net.

Gravity is only one of the forces at work when you play sports or use motion in other ways. Each push, pull, or turn is a force. Try to name the forces this player is using.

Keep Your Balance

Have you ever watched two football players pushing against each other? If each player pushes the other with the same force, they are in balance. Neither one moves. If one pushes with more force, then the other one may fall over.

Sometimes football players use equal force against each other. These forces can also come from opposite directions. When this happens, a balanced force is created.

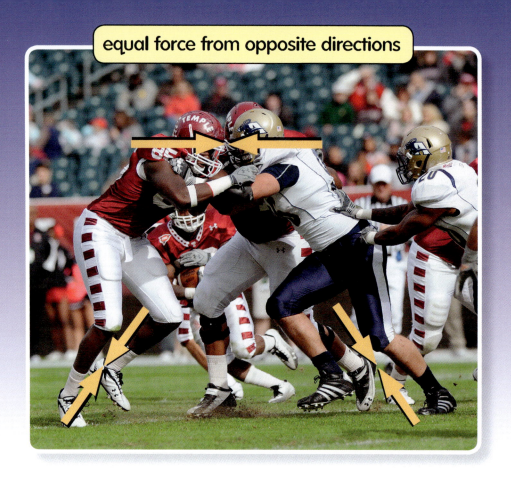

equal force from opposite directions

As the football players push their feet against the ground, the ground also pushes back with an equal force. If the ground is wet, the players' feet will sink in the dirt or mud until the force is balanced.

Whether you play sports, ride your bike, or even write a letter—it's all motion. You can notice how motion happens, and you have the ability to make motion happen. All you have to do is get moving!

Index

balance, 13, 14

basketball, 11

directions, 6, 7, 9, 13

football, 13, 14

forces, 6–14

golf balls, 8–9

gravity, 9–12

gymnasts, 4

inertia, 7–9

motion, 2–4, 6–10, 12, 15

   in a circle, 6

   in space, 10

   laws of, 3, 7

skateboards, 2

speed, 2, 4, 7, 9

teeball, 7

velocity, 4, 7, 9